Herbs 101

A Guide to Growing & Using Herbs

by

Jim Long

Published by

Long Creek Herbs, Inc.
P.O. Box 127
Blue Eye, MO 65611

LongCreekHerbs.com

ISBN 978-1-889791-00-5

Introduction to Growing & Using Herbs

Growing herbs is one of the most relaxing and rewarding activities I can imagine. What other kind of project soothes the soul, brightens the spirit, exercises the body, inspires the neighbors, improves both your health and your landscape, raises property values, and still puts the amazing flavor of healthy foods on your table?

Your herb garden can be your own personal expression, a private spot for meditation, or a family project. Your herb garden can be as small as a patio planter or as big as a field - the choice is yours. Your garden can be simple and precise, or elaborate and wildly imaginative.

Before beginning your garden, decide how you plan to use the herbs from your garden. Admittedly, most people getting into herbs are interested in the culinary herbs to cook with, but the possibilities don't nearly stop there. You could have a fragrance garden for sharing with birds and butterflies. You might want a cosmetic or medicinal herb garden to grow herbs for beauty and health. Or perhaps you imagine a tea garden, or a pizza garden for your kids or grandkids. There are so many options, and all of them good. You'll delight in discovering many of your herbs are multi-purpose.

Your herb garden can be planned on a shoestring budget or carried out on a grand and elegant scale. The plants and seeds cost almost nothing; the ideas are free. The highest costs will likely come from how you carry out your design. In the following pages I offer several simple design ideas for you to choose from and expand upon in your own garden.

Regardless of how you choose to grow your herbs, don't be intimidated. Learn as you go, and make it fun!

The Kitchen Garden

"Want relaxation and inspiration? It's all in your own back yard!" ...C. L. Fornari, Host of the popular *Gardenline* Radio Show.

Before deciding what you want to grow in your kitchen herb garden, consider the following questions:

1. Do you cook often or only occasionally?

2. How much growing space do you have?

3. What kinds of food do you like to eat - Asian, Hispanic, German, Southern, Vegan, Italian, etc.?

4. Do you want an occasional dash of flavor to dress up a simple dish, or do you like to cook entire meals from scratch?

5. What herbs and spices are currently in your spice cabinet? Those are likely the ones you use the most, so do you want fresher versions of the same, or do you want a larger variety?

6. Are you easily intimidated by recipes or are you highly adventurous and likely to try out new dishes?

The answers you give to these questions can help determine how many herbs you want to grow.

The kitchen herb garden is the primary one for many people. The flavor of fresh herbs in home cooked foods can't be equaled from any other source. Your meals will take on a life and sparkle from the fresh-picked herbs you grow. They possess flavors dried herbs can't match.

Kitchen gardens are meant to be as close to the kitchen as possible. When the stew is simmering but the flavor needs just a dash of "something," you should be able to walk outside the door a few steps and snip a few sprigs of rosemary, thyme, sage or oregano to add the finishing touch to your gourmet meal.

There is a direct correlation between the distance from the kitchen to the garden, and how often people use their herbs. If the herb garden is across the lawn or down the hill, you'll use the plants you grow less frequently. But if your kitchen herb garden is just steps away, near a patio or deck, you are much more likely to use your herbs.

Herbs Most Often Found in an American Kitchen Garden

Basil *(Ocimum spp.)* Of the countless varieties to choose from, the most common is sweet basil. Remember to keep the flower stalks snipped out; otherwise it will try to go to seed and the flavor will become bitter. The more you clip and use basil leaves, the better the flavor will be. Basil is an annual herb and you can choose from Lemon, Lime, Thai, Purple and many more kinds.

Chives *(Allium scoenoprasum)* Once you have chives, this hardy perennial will remain for many years. They are a good gateway herb, to get a novice hooked on herb growing.

Dill *(Anethum graveolens)* Dill is a cool season annual, doing very well in spring and early summer, or again in the fall, but will bloom and die in summer. Scatter a few dill seeds every couple of weeks in spring or fall to have plenty on hand.

Garlic Chives *(Allium tuberosum)* This perennial plant tastes like a cross between chives and mild garlic. Beware: it can reseed itself vigorously, so remove seed heads in late summer to keep it in its place.

Lavender *(Lavendula spp.)* This herb has numerous culinary and cosmetic uses. It's a hardy perennial in many parts of the U. S., preferring a raised bed and well-drained soil. Like sage, it does best when cut back by half in very early spring. More common varieties include 'Hidcote' and 'Munstead,' but there are many others available, as well.

Marjoram *(Origanum marjorana)*, sometimes called sweet marjoram. This cold-sensitive perennial is one of the sweetest flavored of the oregano relatives. Grow it in a raised bed or well-drained soil with all day sunshine just as you would oregano. The sweet pine-citrus flavor, with mild oregano accents make this a favorite for pizza and other Mediterranean dishes.

Mint *(Mentha spp.)* Mint is a fast-growing, highly fragrant herb with a rainbow of uses. Spearmint *(Mentha spicata)* is grown from seed, divisions or cuttings (a sprig stuck in a glass of water will root in just a few days). You will find an array of mint flavors, from apple to candy, lime or margarita, all with citrus undertones.

Peppermint, on the other hand, never, ever produces seed so it must always be started from either a cutting or a root division. Any of the mints will grow in full sun to part shade and prefer moist conditions. Don't grow different mint varieties together or they will blend and lose their individuality.

Oregano *(Origanum spp.)* There are many varieties of oregano, some better than others. If you buy oregano seed, you will likely get what's termed, "wild oregano" *(Origanum spp.)*. One of the characteristics of this oregano, is it's invasive, creeping across the herb bed into other plants' spaces much like mint does. If you want a good flavored oregano that works well in a variety of foods, then look for either of these varieties: Greek oregano *(Origanum vulgare hirtum)*, or Kaliteri *(Origanum 'Kaliteri')*. These are not invasive (meaning spreading vigorously by roots). They usually have white flowers and a very pleasant, sweet, oregano flavor and will thrive in well-drained soil in a sunny spot and should live for many years in your garden.

Parsley *(Petroselinum crispum)* Don't be surprised when your parsley returns for a second year. This is a biennial, meaning it grows and produces leaves the first year but blooms then dies the second. Plant this as an annual every year because the second year, the leaves become bitter. If you have room to spare, leave last year's parsley to attract black swallowtail butterflies. The little black, white and yellow striped caterpillars spend part of their life cycle on parsley, fennel or dill, before turning into the lovely butterflies we like in our gardens.

Rosemary *(Rosemarinus officinalis)* Hardy and evergreen in Zones 6b and warmer, rosemary can also be grown as an annual (or dug and moved indoors) if it's not hardy in your area. Two of the more hardy varieties are 'Hill Hardy' and 'Arp.' Plant your rosemary in well-drained soil where it will receive all-day sunlight. Occasionally run your hands over your rosemary plant and breath deeply of its fragrance when working in your garden to refresh and inspire you.

Sage *(Salvia officinalis)* Sage is a hardy perennial which will last for many years, especially if you cut it back by half every spring to keep the plant more robust. Like lavender and thyme, sage does well in raised beds or berms and requires all-day sunshine.

Thyme *(Thymus spp.)* Thyme loves sunny raised beds or pots where it can trail down over the sides. It's a hardy perennial and should grow easily for many years. Thyme is available in several so-called "flavors" including caraway, lemon, orange spice, nutmeg and many others. More upright thyme varieties include French or English thyme, and are also excellent culinary herbs which grow more like small, 6 or 8 inch high "bushes."

Requirements for Growing Culinary Herbs

1. All culinary herbs require 7-10 hours of sunlight each day, and ample sunlight is the most important aspect of where you choose to plant your herb garden. None of the herbs listed above will thrive in shade. Give up now if you want to grow a kitchen garden in your shady back yard.

2. Herbs must have well-drained soil (with the exception of mint, which likes moisture). A raised bed, or a patio planter or pot is perfect. Both methods keep the soil well-drained and prevent roots from sitting in too much moisture in winter.

3. Herbs don't require much in the way of fertilizer. All of the herbs in the kitchen garden list are native to the Mediterranean, where soil is poor and rocky. If you prepare the soil for your raised bed carefully, mixing in organic matter like peat moss or compost with a small amount of bone meal and lime, your garden beds won't require any additional fertilizer for many years.

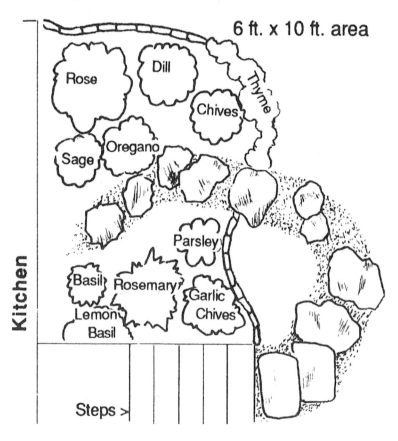

6 ft. x 10 ft. area

Rose · Dill · Chives · Thyme · Oregano · Sage · Parsley · Basil · Rosemary · Garlic Chives · Lemon Basil

Kitchen

Steps >

If you are new to growing herbs, I recommend you start with about 7 the first year. That way you can become accustomed to the flavors more easily. Keep the ones you like the following year, eliminating the ones you don't care for, and adding new ones to try.

A raised bed for herbs can be just 6 or 8 inches above the flat ground. Locate the garden so the growing area isn't under the over-hang of the roof (which stays too dry in summer, and may get too much water from run-off in heavy rains). The soil can be surrounded by rocks, untreated landscape ties, attractive boards or other retaining materials. Railroad ties and treated lumber aren't recommended for making raised beds because the toxic chemicals used to preserve the wood can leach into the soil and be taken up by the plants and eaten by you.

Soil should be tilled or dug up, with organic matter added (peat moss, composted peat moss or similar composted materials are good). Avoid using wood chips in your soil because wood chips consume large amounts of nitrogen as they decompose.

Avoid using water-soluble fertilizers that you apply with a garden hose. Herbs don't need so much fertilizer, and if you do use that kind, you'll get overly rapid growth and little flavor. Also, avoid mixed potting soils that already include chemical fertilizer. The fertilizer is generally too much for growing herbs, and more importantly, many of those also contain pesticides that are meant to be taken up with the fertilizer by the plants to kill off any insect pests.

Mulch

A light application of pine bark (which doesn't leach nitrogen like raw wood chips), is good for keeping weeds out of your beds. Straw works but often holds too much moisture around the herbs. If you live in an area where pine needles are available, those work well, too.

Growing Herbs in Containers or Patio Pots

Patio pots are an excellent way to have an herb garden. You have the ability to move them around to the best location for sunlight, they have good drainage, and they can be grown within a few easy steps of the kitchen. There are many new varieties of herbs and vegetables that are bred especially for patio containers.

When choosing containers for your patio or deck:

1. Look for pots larger than you think you will need. Why? Plants grow, filling the space quickly. Larger pots dry out more slowly than little pots do. A good sized planter to consider is one that is approximately 20 to 24 inches across at the top.

2. When available, choose patio pots which are either double-walled, or made of a hard foam insulating material. This keeps the roots from getting too hot in summer and slows moisture loss.

3. Grow several varieties in one container. For example, parsley, marjoram and chives each take up very little space, so you could grow those 3, plus basil in one 24-inch patio pot.

4. Make sure your patio pot has drainage. If not, drill holes so excess water can drain out

Herbs & Vegetables Bred for Patio Pots

You might consider combining herbs with some of the new mini-vegetable varieties. Here are a few that do well together.

Basil 'Spicy Globe'	Oregano
Basil Container 'Cameo'	Parsley, flat-leaf Italian or curled
Basil 'Mrs. Burns Lemon'	Rosemary
Chives	Sage
Dill 'Dukat'	Thyme
Eggplant 'Little Prince'	Tomato 'Super Bush'
Lettuce 'Garden Babies'	Tomato 'Tiny Tim'
Lettuce 'Tom Thumb' Butterhead	Zucchini Container 'Astia'
Marjoram	

Fill your patio pot with good potting soil, but as I stressed earlier, not the kind with fertilizer and insecticides added. You may want to use a saucer with your patio pot, but it isn't necessary. Consider a coaster with wheels under the pot to make moving it easy.

Plant your herb and/or vegetable plants after all danger of frost has passed. Space the plants 8-10 inches apart in pots to allow them enough room to grow.

You can begin harvesting leaves and sprigs from your herbs when they reach about a foot high. The more often you harvest the leaves of annual herbs, the better the flavor of the new growth will be.

Most people, when first learning to grow herbs, are timid about trimming. They feel guilty for plucking a leaf or two. Keep this in mind if you feel that way:

Many of the culinary herbs we use in the United States are native to areas of the world where historically there were goats or sheep grazing. Every few weeks the goats would come past the oregano, basil or thyme, and eat about half the plant before moving on. In a few days, the herb plants would start growing new, tasty, tender and fresh leaves. So the best thing you can do for your herbs is to either use them a lot, or take a pair of scissors and shear them every 2 or 3 weeks. If you neglect to harvest them, you'll lose their best flavors.

> "The man around the corner keeps experimenting with new flowers
> every year, and now has quite an extensive list of things he can't
> grow." ~William Vaughn

Fragrance & Butterfly Garden

Fragrance gardens are useful and fun because there's so much you can do with fragrant herbs and flowers (for lots of ideas, see my books, **Fabulous Herb & Flower Sorbets, Making Herbal Dream Pillows** and **Herbal Cosmetics** for lots of recipes using flowers and herbs). Fragrance gardens attract butterflies to the garden; bees and hummingbirds will be frequent visitors. Roses and violets can be used in foods, medicines and, crafts can also be a centerpiece of the fragrance garden. All herb flowers, including pineapple sage, French marigolds, basil, lavender, thyme, sage, and others, are fun additions to salads and other foods, as well in potpourris, sleep pillows and bouquets. You'll find a myriad of uses for the plants you grow in a fragrance garden.

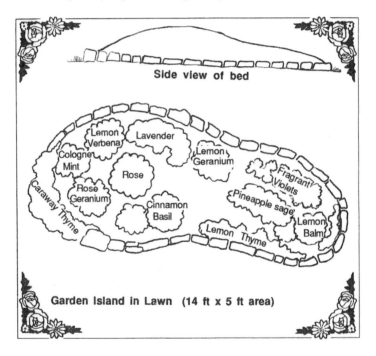

Side view of bed

Garden Island in Lawn (14 ft x 5 ft area)

Consider these in your fragrance garden.

Anise Hyssop (*Agastache foeniculum*) Mildly anise-scented flowers attract bees and butterflies. It's also a tea and culinary herb.

Basil (*Ocimum spp.*) Just look at the names of various basil varieties and you'll get an idea of the fragrances and flavors: 'Cinnamon,' 'Lemon,' 'Lime,' and 'Spicy Globe' among others. Generally thought of as a cooking herb, basil is also a deliciously scented plant.

Lavender *(Lavendula spp.)* Lavender flowers are a fragrant addition to sleep pillows, bouquets and even in the clothes dryer instead of softener sheets. Simply running your fingers over the flowers on a summer evening leaves a soothing fragrance on your skin.

Lemon Balm *(Melissa officinalis)* This is a favorite herb because of its many uses in teas, cakes and cookies. It has mild anti-depressive qualities when used in tea and in sleep pillows. Butterflies love it, and it's a delightful emerald green addition to the garden. Melissa is a hardy perennial and must be clipped often to keep the lemon-scented leaves producing. Prune out seed stalks in fall to keep it from reseeding.

Lemon Thyme *(Thymus citriodorus)* This small creeping perennial loves to grow around the edges of rocks in the garden. The highly-fragrant and lemon-flavored leaves are used in cooking, but more importantly, lemon thyme isn't damaged by being walked on between stepping stones where it releases its delicious aroma.

Lemon Verbena *(Aloysia citrodora)* A tender perennial, but grow it as an annual. This highly-fragrant, lemony scented plant makes a delicious hot or iced tea and is delicious when used used in potpourri blends. Even a small bowlful of leaves will scent a room.

Pineapple Sage *(Salvia elegans)* has enticing pineapple-scented leaves and bright red flowers that hummingbirds love. Rub your fingers over the leaves to release the scent.

Roses *(Rosa spp.)* - All fragrant rose flowers and petals are good to use in cakes, candies, sorbets and ice creams (see my book, **How to Eat a Rose** for recipes). The most enticing quality, however, is the fragrance. In bouquets, sleep pillows, potpourris and even in salads, roses are a delight to the senses. (Just be sure, when eating roses, they haven't been sprayed with insecticides).

Scented Geraniums *(Pelargonium spp.)* These plants include the scents of apple, lemon, nutmeg, rose, and many others. Used sometimes in cakes and cookies, they are mostly grown for their fragrance and use in potpourri.

Violets - *(Viola spp.)* All violas are edible (these are not the same as African violets which aren't edible). Some, like Parma violets (*Parma alba*), have delightful fragrance; others a bit less.

As is true of most fragrant herbs, the best flavor and fragrance is found in the middle of a sunny day. The fragrance (and flavor) comes from the essential oils of the plant and the oil is the strongest during mid-day.

🌿 Tea Garden

Tea gardens evoke images of formal afternoon affairs with dainty little tea cakes served by a butler. It doesn't have to be that way! Herbal teas are one of the quick and easy joys of life. You can brew up a hot cup or an iced glassful in minutes and sip it on the way to work. Replace your afternoon cup of stale coffee with an invigorating wake-me-up cup of healthy herb tea such as anise hyssop with mint. Or combine dried lemongrass, chamomile and rose hips for a nice blend. Add honey or sugar if desired.

Herb teas are healthy, flavorful and delicious alternatives to caffeinated soft drinks. Because you grow them yourself, the flavor is the freshest available anywhere, without any chemicals, preservatives or sugars.

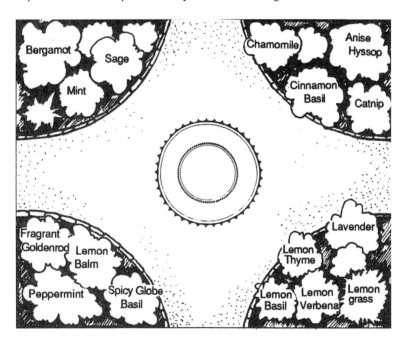

How to brew a good cup of tea:

Start with good water, meaning water free of chemicals or mineral taste. Bring the water to a boil (microwave or stove-top, either one). Put the herbs in a tea infuser, place that in a cup and pour the boiling water over. Place a saucer on top of the cup and leave it there for 5 minutes to keep the fragrant steam from escaping. Remove the infuser and sweeten, or not, and enjoy a hot cup of tea. If you'd rather have iced tea, make a stronger tea and simply fill a glass with ice and pour your freshly-brewed tea over the ice.

Herbs to consider for your tea garden:

Anise Hyssop (*Agastache foeniculum*) A moderately hardy perennial grown for its anise-flavored purple flowers. It's in the larger mint family and spreads somewhat by the roots, but not aggressively. The flower flavor mixes well with lemon verbena, mint, orange peel or chamomile.

Bee-Balm (*Monarda didyma*) Another perennial mint relative, the flowers and sometimes the leaves are used in tea. Choose from several flower colors, all of which have pleasant flavors.

Chamomile (*Matricaria recutita*) The parts used from this annual plant are the tiny daisy-like flowers. The flavor mixes well with may other herbs. Chamomile tea is often used medicinally for treating, insomnia, anxiety and upset stomach. (It was chamomile tea, you may recall, that Peter Rabbit's mother gave Peter after he ate so many carrots he had an upset stomach). Caution: People who have severe allergies to plants, especially ragweed, should avoid this plant. If uncertain, sample cautiously.

Lemon Verbena (*Aloysia citrodora*) A tender perennial valued for its delicious lemony leaves, lemon verbena mixes well with other tea herbs. Just 1 leaf will make a cup of tea.

Catnip (*Nepeta cataria*) A tough and hardy perennial plant that sometimes reseeds itself along the garden borders but is quite easy to grow. Cats love it as a dried herb, and for humans, a cup of catnip tea is a good relaxer and helps with sleep. You can harvest and dry the leaves throughout the summertime.

Lemon Balm (*Melissa officianalis*) Another hardy perennial, lemon balm leaves are delicious in tea blends. Similar to chamomile and catnip, this is a relaxing herb that's good before bedtime as it has anti-depressive and relaxing effects. My favorite way is to brew it the same as "Cold-Pressed Mint Tea" (see page 14) by simply using lemon balm instead of mint. Keep some in the refrigerator where it will keep for 2-3 days and pour into ice-filled glasses for a delicious summertime tea!

Lemongrass (*Cymbopogon citratus*) In tropical regions this is a hardy perennial but for most of the U.S. it's grown as an annual. It will reach 3 feet tall and almost as wide so give it plenty of sunshine and space. This herb likes more moisture than many herbs. Harvest and use the leaves for tea anytime. It is the "bulbs" at the base of the plant that are used in cooking but the leaves are best for tea.

Lavender (*Lavendula spp.*) Lavender is hardy in most areas and must be grown in a raised bed or pot as it requires good drainage. It's another relaxing herb and blends well with lemon-flavored herbs, as well as chamomile, anise hyssop and mint.

Mexican Mint Marigold (*Tagetes lucida*), also known as Mexican tarragon or Texas tarragon; this anise-flavored, tender perennial has a stimulating effect similar to caffein in coffee. Drink it anytime during the day but not in the evening unless you want to stay awake!

Mint (*Mentha spp.*) Mint is a hardy perennial and can be invasive if you allow it to be. Mint leaves are perfect for teas. If growing more than one variety of mint, grow them in different locations because if grown together, the flavors meld and lose their distinctive qualities.

Sweet Woodruff (*Galium odoratum*) A perennial that enjoys both sun and shade. The leaves, with or without flowers, are gathered and dried, then steeped in white wine for a refreshing cold beverage known as "May Wine," once the beverage of choice for springtime weddings.

Cold-Pressed Mint Tea

Here's my favorite way to make iced mint tea: Gather a big handful of any kind of mint, leaves and stems, too. Wring them together like you were wringing a dishcloth. Drop the wadded-up mint into the bottom of a pitcher. Fill that pitcher with ice, all the way to the top. Then fill the pitcher, over the ice, with water. Let it steep for 5 minutes or more, and pour. This is so refreshing you may drink the whole pitcher yourself!

🌿erb Propagation

Herbs can be propagated in many ways. Many, like basil, lemongrass and anise hyssop, can be started from seed. Others like rosemary, thyme, mint, sage, hyssop and winter savory, are faster and easier to start from cuttings. Still others, including bee-balm, mint, lemon balm, some thymes, oregano, even lemongrass, are easy to start by root division.

Don't buy these seeds:

French tarragon (Artemisia dracunculus) - This herb never sets seed, although it rarely may bloom. If you find "tarragon" seed for sale, don't bother buying any because it will be Russian tarragon (Artemisia dracunculoides), also known as false tarragon. False tarragon is bitter and not a good choice for culinary uses; it is also aggressive and will spread rapidly by roots. True French tarragon is only propagated by cuttings, never by seed.

Peppermint (Mentha piperita) - While you occasionally may see this wonderful herb listed in a seed catalog, don't be fooled. Peppermint is sterile, meaning it never, ever sets seed. If you want peppermint, it must come from a root division or cutting. Spearmint (Mentha spicata), on the other hand, will set seed and can be grown from seed, cuttings or root division.

Root Division

Dividing herb plants is best done in early spring. Dig the entire clump out of the ground and using a root saw or sharp spade, cut the clump into several pieces. You can replant each piece for a new plant. Herbs often started by root division include: bee-balm, horseradish, mint, lemon balm, some oregano varieties, Mexican mint marigold and thyme.

Propagating by Cuttings

Herbs that reproduce well by cuttings include: basil, hyssop, horehound, lavender, lemon verbena, French tarragon, mint, oregano, winter savory, rosemary, sage, scented geraniums and thyme. Those can be stuck into damp sand or vermiculite in containers or seed flats.

To root cuttings, prepare a seed flat or flat pan with drainage holes, about 2 inches deep, filled with rooting material - vermiculite, sterilized sand or sterile potting soil. Moisten it well, then smooth it flat and gently firm it down with your hand. With the end of a pencil, make a hole into the soil material, ready for your first cutting.

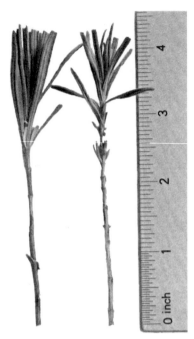

Cuttings ready for sticking in rooting compound.

While cuttings can be taken any time, spring to early summer are the more common times to start them. Cut a sprig of the plant 3-4 inches long. Strip off all the side leaves up to the top 1/2 inch. Dip the cut end of the sprig in rooting compound (found at garden centers and seed stores). Shake off the excess and stick the cutting into the hole you've already made and firm soil around the stem. Repeat with the remainder of your cuttings, sticking each cutting right next to the previous one. Spray the tops of the cuttings lightly with water. Loosely cover the flat with plastic to hold in humidity. Or, you can mist your cuttings daily. It's important they not dry out from the air. The cuttings will root much faster if you keep them on a seed-starting heat mat, and in good light or under a grow-light. You should begin to see new growth start in 3-4 weeks. Once they begin growing well, in a another 2-3 weeks, transplant the cuttings into individual small pots, one plant to a pot, until they are ready to plant outdoors in the garden. (Cuttings do best if transplanted to a small pot and grown for a few weeks rather than planting them directly into the garden)

Starting Herbs from Seed

Herbs which can be easily started from seed include: anise hyssop, bee-balm, basil, calendula, catnip, chamomile, chervil, chives, cilantro, dill, fennel, feverfew, French sorrel, garlic chives, horehound, lemongrass, marjoram, rue and summer savory. (Oregano isn't included in my list because the best-tasting oregano is usually propagated by cuttings instead of seed).

Buy a seed flat at a garden center or your local nursery. You want the kind that is a plastic flat filled with little plant pots. Or, use anything you have around the house like recycled styrofoam cups, yogurt cups, etc. provided they are clean. Make sure each pot has a hole in the bottom for drainage. Fill with sterilized seed-starting soil (it needs to be sterile, otherwise you may have damping-off, a kind of soil-born disease that causes seedlings to shrivel and die soon after sprouting).

If you do have problems with damping off, brew some chamomile tea, using about 2 tablespoons of dry chamomile for 1 quart of water. Water, or mist, your seedlings with the chamomile tea but don't over-water the seedlings. Too much water can cause damping-off problems, too.

Dampen the soil well and firm it down gently, then put 2 or 3 seeds in each little divided pot or container. If you have a seed-starting heat mat, place the flat on that to speed up the germination. It's a good idea to keep the seed flat covered - some seed flats you buy come with a plastic "greenhouse" cover, but you could also use plastic wrap to keep the soil from drying out.

Place the seed flat in a sunny location or under a grow-light. Don't let the seedlings dry out or get too hot and your seeds should come up, on average, in 2-3 weeks. As they grow, make sure they get all day sunlight, indoors, otherwise they will get "leggy," meaning tall, spindly and unhealthy looking. Lack of good light causes this and a grow-light or adequate sunlight all day is the best solution.

Most herb seeds will germinate in 2-3 weeks but basil may sprout up sooner. Lavender and rosemary, by contrast, may take 3-5 weeks to sprout, which is another good reason to take cuttings of those rather than starting from seed. As soon as the seeds have sprouted and are 1/2 inch high, you can remove the plastic cover or plastic wrap.

When your herb seedlings have their first set of real leaves (as opposed to the 2 that came up first), they can be transplanted into larger pots. Seedlings do better if they are transplanted into slightly larger pots, such as from the seed tray or little cups, into a 3 or 4 inch pot. Don't leave them in the seed starting flat too long or they will become stunted and not grow as well. When your plants are 5-6 inches tall and the danger of frost has passed, plant your new seedlings into the herb garden.

Growing Your Herbs

Once you have your herb plants in raised beds or patio pots, water them to help the roots get established, about once a week. Don't over-water them - meaning don't water every day or you'll encourage mildew or rotting of the leaves. They need to dry out between waterings which encourages the roots to grow deeper. When watering, try to avoid simply walking by with a sprinkler hose and spraying the tops. Water the soil rather than the plant tops and soak it enough once a week that when you stick your finger in the soil, it's damp at least 1-2 inches deep.

"Good gardening is very simple, really. You just have to learn to think like a plant." ~ Barbara Damrosch

Harvesting & Storing Herbs

When to Harvest Herbs

For the best flavor, harvest herbs after the dew has evaporated and before the hottest part of the day. Herbs lose some of their flavor as some of the plants' essential oils evaporate in the hot sun. While there's nothing wrong with harvesting herbs like basil, chives, parsley or others in the cool of the evening (I do it often when cooking dinner) just be aware the flavor won't be as strong or aromatic as it was in earlier in the day.

Herbs have the best flavor if harvested often. Once your herb plant reaches about 12 to 15 inches tall, you can safely take up to one third of the plant without harming it, and it will quickly re-grow with fresh, tasty new leaves.

Basil should be harvested often. Use scissors rather than pinching a leaf here and there. Many varieties of basil are prone to flowering and when the plant starts producing flowers, the flavor of the leaves become bitter and less desirable. The more you clip and harvest basil, the better the flavor. If you grow lemon or lime basil, both of those start flowering early and if you don't keep the flowering tops clipped off, about once a week, the plant will go to seed, drop its leaves and die. To prevent that, use your scissors often and dry the clippings.

For mature, established herb plants such as rosemary, savory, sage and thyme, don't harvest more than one third of the plant at a time, in order for the plant to recover.

Preserving the Herbs You Grow

There are many methods for preserving the herbs you've grown for use later. The most common methods are drying or freezing, but they can also be preserved in vinegars, herb jellies and herb oils.

Drying herbs is an excellent way for preserving them for cooking, teas or crafts later. There's no mystery to drying herbs, just simple methods you can easily use. The fastest and simplest method, if you already have a food dehydrator, is to use that. Remove most of the stems of the herbs before drying because the stem contains moisture and will slow down the drying. However if you are drying thyme, rosemary or similar woody, small-leaf herbs, leave the stems in place. Spread the herbs over the dehydrator shelf in one layer, repeating on other shelves and dial the heat setting to low or medium. The herbs should dry until they are brittle and crumble easily. Basil, cilantro and parsley, in particular, should be dried on the lowest heat setting, around 100 degrees Fahrenheit; other herbs can be dried on a medium heat setting.

While some books insist you must wash your herbs before drying them, it is counter-productive. Unless you have a very dirty garden, or chickens and pigs roaming through, your herbs are clean enough to put in the dryer directly from the garden. By washing them, you add additional moisture that simply slows down the drying process and you also wash away some of the important plant oils that give the herb its flavor. If you have a choice and your herbs are without insects, don't wash them before putting them in the dryer.

The perfect place for drying herbs, if anyone had such things anymore, is a dry, dark attic. Herbs need air circulation, darkness and moderate heat to dry well and attics provide all of that. If you have an attic, you can tie your herbs in bundles and hang them in the darkness where they should be dry in about a week and ready to store in air-tight containers.

However, since most houses don't have old-fashioned attics, it's necessary to find something that provides a similar environment. Oddly enough, the back seat or the trunk of a car is the next best thing.

To turn your vehicle into an efficient herb dehydrator, first gather a couple of large handfuls of freshly-picked herbs. Place those in a brown paper grocery bag, fold over the top and clip it closed with a clothes pin or large clip. Repeat with more bags if you're drying several herbs at once. Place the bag(s) in either the trunk of your car, or the floorboard behind the driver's seat. Go about your business, going on errands, etc. If you think of it, shake the bag lightly every 2 or 3 days so the herbs don't settle into a little clump. In a week to 10 days, check the herbs. If they're dry and crispy, take them out of the bags and store them in air-tight containers in the pantry. Most dried herbs will keep for 9-10 months if stored in a dry area without light.

The worst ways to dry herbs are:

1 - Hanging them in a cute bundle in the kitchen. This is fine for decoration but the light in the kitchen, along with cooking smells, will destroy the herb flavor quickly.

2 - Microwaving was once the trendy way to dry herbs. It is the worst of all methods! The microwave does, indeed, dry your herbs, but it also vaporizes the essential oils that give the herbs their flavor - which is why the air smells so good and herby when you open the microwave door. What you have left after microwaving herbs for drying is no better in flavor than dry grass clippings from the lawn!

Storing Your Herbs

Once you have dried your herbs completely and they are crisp enough to crumble, store them in air-tight containers such as jars or zipper bags. Keep the stored herbs in a dark place such as a pantry or cupboard. Dried herbs will keep their flavor and fragrance for up to 9 months, although parsley and basil will lose half of their flavors in about 6 months.

To Store Fresh-Cut Herbs

Whole herb sprigs can be rinsed and the excess moisture shaken off, then placed in a zipper plastic bag with a lightly dampened paper towel. Zip the bag closed and the herbs will remain fresh for about a week. Herbs that store best this way include basil, chives, parsley, French tarragon and garlic chives.

For Storing Fresh Herbs Long-Term

Freezing is a storage method that works well for many herbs. You can pick fresh herbs from the garden and put them in zipper-plastic bags, press out the extra air and seal them. I like to place that bag inside a second bag, pressing out that air, as well. Store them in the freezer for 1-2 months and take them out as you need them. Herbs that freeze well this way include: basil, chives, dill, garlic chives, marjoram, oregano, parsley, rosemary and thyme. Some herbs will freezer burn more quickly than others, so basil and parsley both should be used in 1-2 months.

Another handy way to freeze herbs is to finely chop the herbs in a food processor with a bit of cooking oil, then freeze in ice cube trays. An alternative method is to finely chop the herbs, fill the ice cube trays with the chopped herbs then pour enough water over to finish filling the ice cube container. Either method will preserve much of the flavor and you can drop the cubes as needed, into soup or other dishes during cooking. Herbs that work best with either of these methods include basil, chervil, cilantro, chives, dill and parsley. Store cubes in zipper bags in the freezer.

*See the recipe for my easy frozen pesto recipe on page 26.

Recipes

Don't be afraid to use your herbs when you cook. If you're new to using fresh herbs, introduce yourself to the flavors one at a time. An easy way is chop up an individual fresh herb and mix it with cream cheese. Taste it on a plain cracker to see what the herb tastes like. Another time, chop some of the same herb and mix it into scrambled eggs so you'll get a sense of the herb flavor. Do that with all of your herbs that you aren't familiar with, which should give you more courage for using those flavors in the dishes you cook. Following are some easy recipes using the herbs you've grown.

Bacon Horseradish Dip with Lemon Thyme

This is a tasty dip for fresh vegetables or chips and can be made ahead of time. Lemon thyme adds a nice hint of lemon flavor that blends well with the other ingredients.

6 strips crisp bacon, crumbled

3 green onions, chopped fine (or 2 tablespoons chives)

8 oz. container sour cream

1/2 cup real mayonnaise

3 tablespoons prepared or creamed horseradish

1 tablespoon fresh parsley, chopped fine

1/2 teaspoon fresh lemon thyme, stems removed

1 teaspoon fresh lemon juice

1/2 teaspoon Worcestershire sauce

Combine ingredients and chill until ready to serve. Makes about 2 1/4 cups.

Banana-Basil Smoothie

Use any kind of basil for this - I like Thai, but lemon, sweet, Genovese, Greek Columnar or Purple Ruffles are just as good. In a blender, put 1 frozen banana, 1 tablespoon honey, 7 or 8 basil leaves with 3 cups of milk. Add a few ice cubes and blend everything until it is smooth. For a milk-free smoothie, add pineapple, apple or cranberry-raspberry juice instead.

Basil Grilled Shrimp

Gather a double handful of basil stems with leaves, dip them in water, then spread them loosely on a medium-hot barbecue grill. Spread a layer of raw shrimp over the basil, cover it with foil or grill cover and leave it for about 90 seconds, or until the shrimp turns slightly pink. Turn the shrimp over and leave it for that long again. The flavor of the basil steams into the shrimp. I especially like Lemon or Lime basil for this but any variety will add great flavor.

Bee-Balm Melon Salad

Monarda, or bee-balm, goes especially well with fruits and melons. Any of the bee-balms will work for this and the flower petals add a nice touch of color.

1 honeydew, rind & seed removed, cut into bite-sized pieces

1 cantaloupe, rind & seed removed, cut into bite-sized pieces

6 cups watermelon, in bite-sized pieces

1 cup seedless white grapes, cut in half

1/4 cup any color bee-balm flower petals

2 tablespoons honey

Combine ingredients, tossing lightly. Refrigerate overnight for flavors to meld. Garnish with additional bee-balm petals.

Bruschetta

Serve this with salad, or as an easy appetizer by itself. It's delicious and so simple you can make it for a light and quick summer lunch.

6-7 Roma or sauce-type tomatoes, finely diced

2 cloves garlic, minced

1 green onion, diced

1 teaspoon fresh marjoram leaves

1 tablespoon olive oil

1 teaspoon balsamic vinegar

8-10 fresh basil leaves, finely chopped

Salt & freshly-ground black pepper

Extra olive oil for the bread

6-10 medium-thick slices French bread

1. Mix together the ingredients except for the extra olive oil and French bread. This mixture can be set aside for up to 2 hours before serving time - this is best served at room temperature. Drain.

2. Spread olive oil on top of medium-thick slices of French bread and toast them under the broiler until bread starts to brown at the edges.

3. Top each slice generously with the herb and tomato mixture and serve while the toast is still warm. Serves 4-6.

> *"There can be no other occupation like gardening in which, if you were to creep up behind someone at their work, you would find them smiling."* ~Mirabel Osler

Calendula-Marjoram Cornbread Muffins

These are way too good to serve with margarine. Serve them with real butter!

1 cup yellow cornmeal

3/4 cup whole wheat or unbleached flour

2 teaspoons baking powder

1/2 teaspoon salt

2 eggs

1 cup milk

3 tablespoons cooking oil

3/4 cup grated extra-sharp cheddar cheese

1 cup fresh or frozen corn

1/4 cup dry, or 1/2 cup fresh, calendula petals (stem and green parts removed; If you use dry petals, cover them with 1/4 cup boiling water and let them soften for 5 minutes. Squeeze out as much water as you can before using in the recipe).

1 teaspoon fresh marjoram leaves

1. Preheat oven to 375 degrees F. then oil a 12-section muffin pan.

2. Combine dry ingredients in mixing bowl and stir to mix.

3. In a second bowl, beat together the eggs, milk and oil, then pour into the dry ingredients, mixing well.

4. Stir in the calendula petals, marjoram and corn, mixing again.

5. Spoon into the greased muffin pan, filling 3/4 way to the top. Bake for 20 minutes or until golden brown. Makes about 8-12 muffins, depending upon the size of your muffin pan.

When using calendula, use petals, discarding green parts.

Chilled Lettuce Soup

This is an excellent light summer lunch or you might serve it as the soup portion of an elegant dinner. Either way, it is delicious! (This soup also pairs well with either the Bruschetta or the Calendula-Marjoram Muffins, above).

2 tablespoons butter or olive oil	2 cups water
1 medium yellow onion, diced	1 teaspoon freshly-picked marjoram leaves
2 to 3 heads butterhead or Romaine lettuce, coarsely sliced	1 cup half-and-half or heavy cream
2 cups chicken or vegetable stock	Salt & pepper to taste

1. Sauté onions in butter for about 2 minutes. Add nearly all of the lettuce, saving back about 1/4 cup for garnish. Stir the lettuce until it wilts.

2. Add the chicken stock and bring to a boil, then lower heat to a simmer and cook for 5 minutes or until lettuce is soft. Add the marjoram leaves.

3. Process in a blender with 2 cups of water until smooth. Refrigerate for an hour or even overnight.

4. Add the half-and-half just before serving. Serve chilled, in small bowls, and garnish with the reserved lettuce, sliced into tiny ribbons, along with a marjoram sprig. For more color, add shredded red radishes to the garnish. Serves 4-6.

Dill Dip

Serve this with chips or fresh vegetables.

1 cup sour cream	1 green onion, diced fine (or 1 tablespoon chives)
3/4 cup real mayonnaise	3 tablespoons freshly-chopped dill leaves
2 cloves garlic, peeled and minced	Salt to taste

Mix well and refrigerate for at least an hour or overnight, until ready to serve. Makes 1 3/4 cups.

"God made rainy days so gardeners could get the housework done."
~Author Unknown

Freezer Pesto

Here's an easy recipe for using basil in summer. While basil dries well, the best, nearest to fresh flavor comes from making pesto from the fresh leaves and freezing that for later. I've shared this method with friends many times and they say they love the results.

4 cups basil leaves, loosely packed

1 cup extra virgin olive oil

4 tablespoons pine nuts, almonds or walnuts

6 cloves garlic, peeled

1 tablespoon freshly-squeezed lemon juice

1/2 teaspoon salt

*1/3 cup Romano cheese, added later

*1/3 cup Parmesan cheese, added later

1. Put everything into the food processor and blend the ingredients until you have a smooth paste. Scrape the edges to make sure everything has been processed.

2. Pour the mixture into ice cube trays, filling each section. Freeze for 24 hours, then pop out the cubes into zipper plastic bags and keep them frozen until you are ready to use some.

3. Weeks or months later, when you are ready to use your pesto, combine it with half Romano, half Parmesan cheese, freshly grated if possible. Since those cheeses don't freeze well, the flavor of your pesto will stay much fresher if you don't put the cheese in the pesto before freezing.

Herb vinegars

Herb vinegars are made by putting a few sprigs of fresh herbs into a bottle and filling that with vinegar. Making herb vinegars is a good way to keep the flavors to use in salad dressings later. Herbs that work well in vinegars include: chive blossoms with oregano, French tarragon with peppercorns, oregano and garlic, lemon basil with thyme, garlic and rosemary - there are endless combinations for making tasty herb vinegars. (For lots of recipes for making herb vinegars, consult my book, **Making Herb Vinegars**, available on my website). Here's one from that book.

The best vinegars to use for making good quality herb vinegars include these: rice, apple cider, champagne, white wine and red wine; the least desirable vinegar to use is white distilled.

Lemony-Herb Vinegar

This is good on grilled or broiled seafood. It also makes a versatile low-calorie salad dressing ingredient, or a light salad dressing by itself.

2 4-inch sprigs lemon balm (or 1 tablespoon dry)

4 4-inch sprigs lemon basil (or 2 tablespoons dry)

2 4-inch sprigs spearmint (or 1 tablespoon dry)

Piece of fresh lemon peel, about 1/2 inch wide, 2 inches long, white pith removed

1 quart white wine vinegar or similar favorite vinegar

1. Combine ingredients in a quart glass jar, covered with plastic wrap or noncorrosive lid. Set aside on the kitchen counter for 2 weeks, gently shaking every day.

2. Strain, discarding herbs, bottle in a decorative bottle and add a fresh sprig of each herb for decoration. This doesn't need to be refrigerated and will keep for up to 6 months. Makes 4 cups.

Herbed Cheese Appetizer

I hosted an Herb Day in May festival at my herb farm for many years and this appetizer was always a hit. I often serve this to guests before dinner.

1 pound mozzarella or farmer's cheese, cut into bite-sized pieces

2 tablespoons olive oil

1 tablespoon freshly-chopped marjoram

4 tablespoons freshly-chopped parsley

2 tablespoons freshly-chopped chives or garlic chives

1 teaspoon celery leaves, optional

Combine the herbs and oil in a medium-sized bowl and mix, then add the herb cubes and gently mix to coat. Refrigerate a few hours or overnight, drain and serve with toothpicks and crackers. Serves 6-10 as an appetizer or hors d'oeuvre.

Herb Butters

Herb butters are great for spreading on thick-sliced fresh bread or toast. Try them with hot dinner rolls or use one to rub over the turkey before baking at Thanksgiving. There are so many great uses for herb butters and so many kinds you can make. Consider one or a combination of the following: basil, chives, dill, garlic, garlic chives, marjoram, oregano or rosemary. Combine 2, such as garlic and marjoram for an outstanding garlic toast.

Start with 1/2 cup (one stick) of real butter, at room temperature.

Chop the herbs fairly fine to make 2 heaping tablespoons of fresh herbs. Mix into the butter, stirring until well combined. Line a small bowl, about 1 cup size, with plastic wrap, then scrape the soft butter into the bowl. Cover the bowl with plastic wrap and refrigerate for a day or more. Turn the bowl upside down onto a small plate and pull off the plastic wrap. Garnish with fresh herbs and serve. Refrigerate any left over for use in cooking, or freeze for later.

Herb Butter with Lemon Zest

1/4 cup mixed herbs, such as flat-leaf parsley, chervil, tarragon, and chives, chopped fine	1 cup (2 sticks) unsalted butter, softened
	1 teaspoon finely grated lemon zest

Combine ingredients, mixing well. Cover with plastic wrap and refrigerate until ready to use. This is good rubbed on chicken before grilling, as well as delicious on fresh-baked bread or even your morning toast.

Italian Seasoning

This blend is delicious when making pizza sauce, spaghetti sauce or other Italian dishes. Store in an air-tight container in the pantry. All herbs should be dry enough to crush easily.

2 tablespoons oregano	2 tablespoons parsley
2 tablespoons marjoram	2 teaspoons garlic powder or granules
2 tablespoons basil	

To use, add 1 or more tablespoons to the sauce while cooking.

> *"Plants give us oxygen for the lungs, and for the soul."*
> *~Linda Solegato*

Lemon Balm Cookies

These are my favorite quick and easy cookies and guests nearly always ask for more. You can freeze these and keep them for about a month in the freezer, but they're so easy you can make a fresh batch any time.

1 cup (2 sticks) butter, softened	1 teaspoon vanilla extract
1 1/2 cups sugar	2 1/2 cups flour
2 eggs	1/4 cup coarsely chopped lemon balm leaves
1/2 teaspoon lemon extract	
1/2 teaspoon salt	2 teaspoons baking powder

1. Preheat oven to 350 degrees F.

2. In a food processor, put 1 cup of the sugar and the lemon balm leaves. Pulse-process until the lemon balm leaves are well chopped.

3. Add the remaining sugar and the butter and process until fluffy. Add remaining ingredients and pulse-process until well combined.

4. Drop by small spoonfuls onto a greased baking sheet (or parchment paper on a baking sheet), leaving about 2 inches between cookies. Bake for 8-10 minutes, or until edges just begin to brown. Loosen from cookie sheet while still warm and cool. Makes 15-20 cookies, depending on the size.

Lemon Balm, Lemon Thyme Blueberry Cake

A popular dessert I served at my Herb Day in May festivals. Lemon thyme can be harvested the year around as it is evergreen and hardy in many areas.

3/4 cup milk

4 tablespoons fresh lemon balm leaves chopped

3 tablespoons fresh lemongrass leaves, snipped fine (or 1 1/2 tablespoons dry)

1 tablespoon fresh lemon thyme, larger stems removed

2 cups flour

1 1/2 teaspoons baking powder

1/4 teaspoon salt

2 eggs

1 cup sugar

6 tablespoons butter, room temperature

Grated lemon zest from one whole lemon

2 cups fresh or frozen, thawed & drained blueberries

1. Preheat oven to 350 degrees F.
2. Heat milk to almost boiling, then pour milk into a food processor and add the lemon balm, lemongrass, and lemon thyme. Process until herbs are chopped fine. Set aside to allow hot milk to draw out the flavors of the herbs.
3. Combine flour, baking powder, and salt.
4. Mix together milk-herb mixture and flour mixture.
5. Add eggs, sugar, butter, and lemon zest, mixing well. Fold in the blueberries.
6. Pour mixture into greased 9-inch by 5-inch bread pan. Bake for about 50 minutes or until a toothpick comes out clean.
7. While still hot, prick the top of the cake with a knife or chopstick several times and pour the glaze slowly over to let it soak in. Cool well before serving.

Glaze:

1. Combine juice of 4 lemons with 3/4 cup powdered sugar. Mix well until sugar is dissolved, then pour over still hot cake, allowing it to soak in, repeat until all the glaze is used up.

Lemon Verbena Whipped Cream

1 pint whipping cream

4 fresh lemon verbena leaves

2. Crush leaves a bit in your hands, then add to the whipping cream.
3. Cover and refrigerate over-night.
4. The following day, remove leaves and beat the whipping cream until it forms stiff peaks. Add 2 teaspoons powdered sugar near the end of the beating process. Serve on fresh strawberries, blueberries or blackberries.

Nasturtium Cheese Spread

Nasturtium flowers are also delicious seasoning herbs: chop 4 or 5 nasturtium flowers and mix them with 3 ounces of room temperature cream cheese, then spread it on your favorite crackers for a tasty snack.

Poultry Seasoning

You can easily make your own poultry seasoning from the herbs you've grown and it will be fresher than what you buy in the store. The herbs should be well-dried and crumble easily. Use 2-3 teaspoons or more, in sage dressings as well as when boiling or roasting chicken or turkey. In general, when making soups or stews, add the herb near the end of cooking, usually in the last 10-15 minutes of cooking time, for the best flavor.

1/4 cup sage	1/4 cup rosemary
1/4 cup marjoram	2 tablespoons thyme

Place herbs in a blender and pulse-blend until fine. Store in air-tight container. Makes 3/4 cup.

Rosemary-Orange Chocolate Chip Cookies

I came up with this recipe to use in a kids' cooking class. It's a good way to introduce kids, or even novice adults, to the flavor of rosemary by combining the herb with 2 favorites: chocolate and oranges.

2 sticks (1 cup) butter, softened	1 teaspoon vanilla extract
1 teaspoon baking soda	2 eggs
1 teaspoon salt	2 cups (12-oz. pkg.) semi-sweet chocolate chips
2 1/4 cups flour	
3/4 cup granulated sugar	2-3 teaspoons chopped fresh rosemary leaves
3/4 cup packed brown sugar	Grated orange peel from 1 orange

1. Preheat oven to 375 degrees F.
2. Mix flour, baking soda and salt in small bowl and set aside
3. Beat butter, granulated sugar, brown sugar and vanilla in large mixing bowl until creamy.
4. Add eggs and beat.
5. Add flour mixture, stirring well.
6. Stir in chocolate pieces, rosemary and grated orange peel.
7. Drop by rounded tablespoons onto baking sheets.
8. Bake for 9 to 11 minutes or until golden brown. Cool on baking sheets for 2 minutes; remove to wire racks to cool completely. Makes about 2 dozen cookies.

Rosemary Lemonade

Once you've made this for your family, they may not want to go back to "ordinary" lemonade. (Fool them with the *Tip below if you don't want to squeeze lemons).

1 1/2 cups water

1 1/2 cups sugar

1 1/2 cups freshly squeezed lemon juice

The empty "shells" of the lemons after you've squeezed out the juice

2 4-inch sprigs of fresh rosemary

1. Combine the water and sugar in a saucepan and bring to a boil. Stir to dissolve sugar.

2. Add remaining ingredients, cool, then refrigerate for at least 2 hours. Remove and discard the rosemary sprigs.

3. To serve, add ice to drinking glasses and pour lemonade to fill. Garnish with a fresh sprig of rosemary. Makes about 3 cups or enough to serve 2-3 people.

ROSEMARY

*Even when you are faced with just a plain can of concentrated lemonade, or the powdered stuff, a few lemon slices and a generous sprig of rosemary will transform it into a delicious beverage.

Salt-Free Oil & Vinegar Salad Dressing

This is a low-calorie, healthy and tasty salad dressing. Double the recipe to store some for later, where it will keep in the refrigerator for up to a week.

1/4 cup herb vinegar (tarragon, chive or what you have on hand)

1/8 cup extra-virgin olive oil

1 tablespoon chopped fresh chives (or 1 green onion)

1 teaspoon marjoram (about one 4-inch sprig, stem removed)

1 garlic clove, peeled

1/2 teaspoon honey or sugar

Dash salt & pepper, to taste

Pour the ingredients into a blender and blend well. Let set for an hour for flavors to combine. Stir or shake before pouring on a mixed greens salad.

Tulips Stuffed with Chicken Salad

Yes, tulip flowers are edible! This makes an elegant lunch in springtime. Remove the tulip stamens (centers) before stuffing.

6 cups cooked, diced chicken or turkey, mostly white meat

2 cups celery, medium-diced

1/8 cup diced fresh chive blossoms or 4 scallions, diced

2 tablespoons fresh garlic chive leaves, chopped

2 tablespoons fresh parsley, chopped fine

1/2 cup (or a 5-ounce can) water chestnuts, drained and coarsely chopped

2 teaspoons fresh marjoram, finely chopped (or 1/2 tsp. poultry seasoning)

1 cup pecans, lightly toasted

1 cup seedless white grapes, cut in halves

4 red radishes, sliced or diced

3/4 cup real mayonnaise (enough to moisten the salad)

Salt and pepper to taste

6-8 whole tulip flowers with short stem left on to hold petals together

1. Combine ingredients, mixing well. Add more mayonnaise if needed. Refrigerate for several hours or overnight.

2. Leave tulips whole but remove the stamen - that's the fuzzy piece in the center.

3. Stuff approximately 1/3 cup of the mixture into each whole tulip. Serve stuffed tulip on its side, on a lettuce leaf with your favorite cracker (or make crackers from my book: ***Easy Homemade Crackers with Herbs***). Serves 6-8

> *"Don't wear perfume in the garden - unless you want to be pollinated by bees."* ~Anne Raver

$\mathbb{M}$ore Uses for Your Herbs

Herbal Bath Blend

Delightful in the bath, or make a bath mitt and fill with the mixture if you only take showers. The herbs are especially relaxing and fragrant, leaving your skin feeling soft and refreshed. Use all dried herbs for this mixture.

1/2 cup calendula flowers	1/4 cup sage
1/2 cup rosemary leaves	1/4 cup thyme
1/4 cup mint	1/4 cup Epsom salt
1/4 cup lavender	

You could also add a few drops of rose or lavender oil if you want more fragrance, but it's not necessary.

1. Mix the ingredients and store in an air-tight container until ready to use.

2. To use: Take out a cupful of bath blend and tie it up in a wash cloth held together with string, or use a cotton drawstring bag.

3. Bring 4 cups of water to a boil and drop in the bag of bath blend. Let steep for 15 minutes while you are filling the tub with warm water. Pour this "tea" into your bath and relax in the pleasant herby-ness. Or if you only shower, slightly wring out the cloth-filled, soaked bag and use it like a bath mitt, gently massaging your body.

Herbal Moth-Repelling Blend

1. Combine 1 cup each (dried) herb: tansy, whole bay leaves and French marigold blossoms. To that, add 6 cups fragrant cedar wood shavings, and 1/2 cup whole allspice berries, 1/2 cup juniper berries and 1/2 cup lavender flowers.

2. Mix together and store in an air-tight container. To use, put 1/2 cup in cotton drawstring bags (or tie in attractive cloth) and hang several in your closet, or place one in each drawer. The fragrance is pleasing to people, but clothes moths flee the aroma of these herbs.

Relaxing Restful Dream Blend

*This mixture is especially good for children or adults who suffer from nightmares. Even soldiers who suffered from flash-back nightmares and PTSD have reported better sleep and fewer nightmares with my dream blend. For more information about dream blends, consult my book, **Making Herbal Dream Pillows** (Storey Publishing) on my website, or visit my Dream Pillows page at LongCreekHerbs.com. (Herb ingredients and ready-made Dream Pillows also available there, as well).*

This makes enough for 2 dream pillows.

1 heaping tablespoon dried rose petals

1 heaping tablespoon dried marjoram

1 heaping tablespoon dried mugwort leaves

1 heaping tablespoon sweet hops

Mix together and place 2 heaping tablespoons of the mixture into a 3 x 5 inch cotton drawstring bag and tie closed. Place that anywhere inside your pillowcase. You should notice more peaceful, restful sleep without dreams or nightmares.

To Candy Violets
(or rose petals, mint leaves or scented geranium leaves)

1. Pick blossoms in the morning after the dew has evaporated but before the heat of the day. Separate an egg, putting the egg white in a small dish and discarding the egg yolk or keeping it for another purpose.

2. With a fork, froth-up the egg white slightly.

3. Dip each violet or blossom into the egg white, shaking off most of the excess.

4. While holding the violet over another small bowl, slowly pour granulated sugar over it, coating top and bottom. Lay the coated violet on a piece of waxed paper on a cookie sheet, and repeat with the remaining flowers.

5. When all the blossoms are coated with sugar and on the waxed paper/cookie sheet, place the cookie sheet in the oven. If your oven has a pilot light, leave the door open and leave the baking sheet-blossoms there until they are dry, about 2 days. Or, if no pilot light, set the oven to 100 degrees F. and let them dry that way. You could also use a food dehydrator, where they will be dry in about 12 hours.

6. To store your candied blossoms, layer them with waxed paper in an air-tight container and store that in a dark, cool place such as a pantry or kitchen cabinet.

Index

The Kitchen Garden 3
Herbs Most Often Found in American Kitchen Garden 4, 5
Requirements for Growing Culinary Herbs 6, 7
Growing Herbs In Containers or Pots 8
Herbs & Vegetables Bred for Patio Pots 9
A Fragrance & Butterfly Garden 10,11
A Tea Garden 12, 13, 14
Herb Propagation 15, 16, 17
Harvesting & Storing Herbs. 18
Preserving the Herbs You Grow 19, 20
Storing Your Herbs 20, 21
Recipes 22
Bacon Horseradish Dip with Lemon Thyme. 22
Banana-Basil Smoothie. 22
Basil Grilled Shrimp 22
Bee-Balm Melon Salad 23
Bruschetta. 23
Calendula-Marjoram Cornbread Muffins 24
Chilled Lettuce Soup. 25
Dill Dip 25
Freezer Pesto 26
Herb Vinegars, Lemony-Herb Vinegar 26,27
Herbed Cheese Appetizer. 27
Herb Butters. 28
Herb Butter with Lemon Zest 28
Italian Seasoning 28
Lemon Balm Cookies 29
Lemon Balm, Lemon Thyme Blueberry Cake. 30
Lemon Verbena Whipped Cream 30
Nasturtium Cheese Spread. 31
Poultry Seasoning 31
Rosemary-Orange Chocolate Chip Cookies 31
Rosemary Lemonade 32
Salt-Free Oil & Vinegar Salad Dressing 32
Tulips Stuffed with Chicken Salad. 33
Herbal Bath Blend. 34
Herbal Moth-Repelling Blend 34
Relaxing Restful Dream Blend. 35
To Candy Violets 35

For Sources of herb plants and seed, visit my website *LongCreekHerbs.com* and look under the "Looking for Plants?" button.

You'll find more recipes and plant stories on my gardening adventures blog: *jimlongsgarden.blogspot.com* or visit my website for my other books and products at *LongCreekHerbs.com*